DOUBLE THE HUMOR . . .

Who legalized marijuana?
A joint session of Congress

Why did the cannibal roast the fortune teller for hours?
He liked his mediums well-done.

Why is Ralph Nader so humorless?
He can't recall jokes.

WITH *DOUBLY GROSS JOKES!*

SPINE TINGLING HORROR
from Zebra Books

CHILD'S PLAY (1719, $3.50)
by Andrew Neiderman
From the day the foster children arrived, they looked up to Alex. But soon they began to act like him—right down to the icy sarcasm, terrifying smiles and evil gleams in their eyes. Oh yes, they'd do anything to please Alex.

THE DOLL (1788, $3.50)
by Josh Webster
When Gretchen cradled the doll in her arms, it told her things—secret, evil things that her sister Mary could never know about. For it hated Mary just as she did. And it knew how to get back at Mary . . . forever.

DEW CLAWS (1808, $3.50)
by Stephen Gresham
The memories Jonathan had of his Uncle and three brothers being sucked into the fetid mud of the Night Horse Swamp were starting to fade . . . only to return again. It had taken everything he loved. And now it had come back—for him.

TOYS IN THE ATTIC (1862, $3.95)
by Daniel Ransom
Brian's best friend Davey had disappeared and already his clothes and comic books had vanished—as if Davey never existed. Somebody was playing a deadly game—and now it was Brian's turn . . .

THE ALCHEMIST (1865, $3.95)
by Les Whitten
Of course, it was only a hobby. No harm in that. The small alchemical furnace in the basement could hardly invite suspicion. After all, Martin was a quiet, government worker with a dead-end desk job. . . . Or was he?

Available wherever paperbacks are sold, or order direct from the Publisher. Send cover price plus 50¢ per copy for mailing and handling to Zebra Books, Dept. 1945, 475 Park Avenue South, New York, N.Y. 10016. Residents of New York, New Jersey and Pennsylvania must include sales tax. DO NOT SEND CASH.

Doubly GROSS JOKES

By Julius Alvin

ZEBRA BOOKS
KENSINGTON PUBLISHING CORP.

ZEBRA BOOKS

are published by

Kensington Publishing Corp.
475 Park Avenue South
New York, NY 10016

First Zebra Books printing: September 1986

Printed in the United States of America

DEDICATION

To Nancy, Ryan's creator and my re-creator.

SPECIAL THANKS

To Eddie Kritzer, producer of the incredibly funny **GROSS JOKES** *video and, more importantly, an honest and talented man in a very tough business—thanks for your faith in this series.*

To Kiki, the baby friend, whose fine care of the Booper helped make this book possible—may your enemies always E.S. & D.

CONTENTS

Chapter One:

DOUBLY GROSS RACIAL
AND ETHNIC JOKES

How can you tell a guy is a regular at a Greek whorehouse?

He's always coming in the rear.

———————————

Why did so many blacks die in Viet Nam?

When their platoon leader yelled, "Get down!", they all got up and danced.

———————————

Why don't Jewish women have any moral qualms about abortion?

They believe that life doesn't begin until medical school.

How do we know Arabs are insatiable lovers?

After screwing one of their wives, they always want a Camel.

Why did eighteen Polacks go to the movies?

Because the sign said, "Under seventeen not admitted."

What do you call a frozen cesspool?

Italian Ice.

A Polish girl walked into the drugstore and asked the pharmacist what he recommended for her husband's dandruff. The pharmacist suggested Head & Shoulders.

Two days later the pharmacist received a call from the girl. "How do you give 'shoulders'?"

What's a formal Italian dinner?

One where all the men come to the table with their flies zipped.

The teacher was quizzing her first grade class about animals. "What sounds does a cow make?" she asked.

A little black boy in the last row stood up. "A cow goes 'Moo'," he said.

"Very good, Leroy," the teacher said. "Now tell the class what sound a sheep makes."

"A sheep goes 'Baaaa'," Leroy replied.

"Wonderful!" the teacher exclaimed. "And what does a pig say?"

Leroy replied, "A pig say, 'Freeze, motherfuckers! Put your hands over your fucking heads!'"

———————————

Why aren't there any Polish bisexuals?

Twice a year isn't enough for them.

———————————

How can you tell if a woman is half-Irish and half-Italian?

She mashes potatoes with her feet.

———————————

What's a Jewish pervert?

A guy who wants to go into his mother's business.

When do Greeks get really turned on at night?

When they see a full moon.

_____

Why don't black children play hide and seek?

Who would come looking for them?

_____

How did the Puerto Rican finally pull off a successful burglary?

The batteries on his radio went dead on the way to the crime.

_____

Why did the pregnant Polish woman have a blood test?

To find out if the baby was really hers.

_____

Why hasn't a Puerto Rican writer ever won the Nobel Prize?

Because the committee won't go to New York to read the side of the A train.

What's a Mexican blow job?

A senorita bends over and farts in your face.

———————————

Why do Italian men like women with big tits and small pussies?

Because Italian men have big mouths and small dicks.

———————————

What's a Jewish porno film?

55 minutes of begging, 5 minutes of sex, and an hour of guilt.

———————————

Why did the Irish Parliament cancel St. Patrick's Day?

They dug up his body and discovered he died of sickle cell anemia.

———————————

How many Polacks does it take to make chocolate chip cookies?

Twenty. One to stir the batter and nineteen to peel the M&M's.

What does a Polack play on his Walkman?

"Left, right, left, right, left, right . . ."

Two Vietnamese refugees were flown to New York City. They expected total culture shock, so it was a huge delight to them to find out that one of New York's favorite foods was the "hot dog."

As soon as they received some money, they eagerly rushed out to a street vender. They received their delicacy, but when the first Vietnamese unwrapped his food, he groaned.

"What's wrong?" his friend asked.

"I'll tell you in a minute. After you tell me what part you got."

How can you tell WASP wives think sex with their husbands is work?

Because most of them let the maid do it.

What's a Polish abortion?

Douching with Drano.

How can you tell if a black kid is smart?

If he can remember the name of the guy that's fucking his mother this week.

―――――――――

How can you tell if a black kid is a genius?

If he can remember the name of the guy that was fucking his mother last week.

―――――――――

Why did the Nazis find it so easy to round up the Jews?

All they had to do was roll a coin down the street.

―――――――――

Why don't Israeli soldiers wear bullet-proof vests?

Because if they don't work, they can't get their money back.

―――――――――

What do you call 1,000 Puerto Ricans pushing shopping carts?

The K-Mart Thanksgiving Day Parade.

Why did the Polish girl remove the mirror over her bed?

She saw a crack in it.

––––––––––––––––––

Did you hear about the new Polish invention?

A solar-powered flashlight.

––––––––––––––––––

Why did the Polish woman stick her head in the freezer?

She wanted to frost her hair.

––––––––––––––––––

Why did the Polack buy an electric lawn mower?

So he could find his way back to the house.

––––––––––––––––––

Why are synagogues round?

So Jews can't hide in the corner when the collection plate comes around.

What's Polish birth control?

Kicking your husband in the shins to make him limp.

—————————

One Polack ran into another on the street and asked, "I thought you had a new job?"

"My pecker was so sore after two days, I had to quit."

The first Polack looked incredulous. "Why was your pecker so sore?"

"Yours would be, too," the second Polack replied, "if they'd given you an office and told you to use your Dictaphone all day long."

—————————

Why did the Harlem grandmother have a hysterectomy?

'Cause she didn't want no more grandchildren.

—————————

Why did the Polish proctologist use 2 fingers?

He wanted a second opinion.

Why did the Polack sell his water skis?

He couldn't find a lake on a hill.

What do you get when you cross 6 million Jews and a German?

A German.

Why don't they have seat belts in new Cadillacs?

Because they've installed Velcro on the ceiling.

Why are there over one billion Chinese?

If you don't know, you've never tried to do your own shirts.

Why do Italian girls wear sleeveless dresses?

They love the feeling of wind blowing through their hair.

Why do blacks have such prominent posteriors?

When God made the first black, he granted the dude one wish. The black asked God, "I wants to get my ass high."

What sign does a black epileptic wear on his chest?

"I am not break dancing."

What kind of video turns on JAP's?

A tape of the fur sales at Bloomingdales.

Why did the Polack strap an ice bag to his nose?

He wanted to keep his lunch cold.

What do you get when you cross a black and a gay Eskimo?

A snow blower that doesn't work.

A Polish scientist was doing research on frogs. He laid a frog on a table, slammed his hand on the table, then yelled, "Jump!" The frog jumped.

Next, he removed one front leg, yelled "Jump!" and again the frog jumped. He removed another front leg and repeated the procedure. This time the frog jumped with difficulty.

Finally, he removed the last two remaining legs, slammed his hand on the table, and yelled, "Jump!" The poor frog remained still.

The doctor wrote in his notes, "It is scientifically proven that when a frog's legs are removed, it goes deaf."

———————

Why did they kick the Polack out of the airport?

He was throwing stale bread to the planes.

———————

What are Greek designer pants for men?

The zipper's in the rear.

———————

Why don't French women care how well-endowed their husbands are?

All pricks taste alike.

Why did the Polack take the used tampon to the museum?

He wanted to find out what period it was from.

———————

Why didn't the Polack try marijuana a second time?

The first time, it hurt too much when he lit his joint.

———————

What's the difference between a JAP and Jaws?

Nail polish.

———————

Why do orgies make WASPs so uncomfortable?

They never know who to thank.

———————

Why did the Polack keep coming back to the movie box office to buy another ticket?

Because some guy at the door kept tearing his in half.

Why did the female black inmate turn down parole?

She didn't want to go to no half-way house—she wanted an all-the-way house.

———————

Why did the Italian plant Cheerios in his garden?

He wanted to grow doughnuts.

———————

Why did the Polish mother dunk her tits in milk?

She wanted to breast feed.

———————

Did you hear about the new business started by the Polish entrepreneur?

Self-service massage parlors.

———————

A Polish teacher asked the boy in the front row, "What's 2 x 2?"
"I don't know," the boy replied.
"That's the right answer," the teacher replied.

Why are there screen doors on Italian submarines?

To keep fish out.

———————————

Why did the Polish musician have welts on the side of his head?

He was trying to play the piano by ear.

———————————

How can you tell a chic Polish woman?

She's wearing open-toed bowling shoes.

———————————

Why is it so easy to catch Polish burglars in the dark?

They wear white bowling shoes.

———————————

What's blacks' favorite summer water sport?

Waterskiing through car washes.

A black from rural Louisiana took a trip to New Orleans. What awed him most was the flashy pimps driving around in their big Cadillacs. He asked his cousin, who lived in New Orleans, how he could be like those fancy dudes.

"First thing," his cousin said, "is you gots to get yourself some alligator shoes."

The black went back home to the bayous. Two weeks later he showed up at his cousin's house in New Orleans, bandaged from head to foot and swearing at the top of his lungs.

"What happened?" the cousin asked.

"Those fucking alligators tore the shit out of me," the black swore. "And on top of that, every ones I catch was barefoot."

————————

Why did the Polack feed his sheep iron supplements?

He wanted them to grow steel wool.

————————

Did you hear about the new lipstick for black women?

It comes with its own paint roller.

Where do Polish hookers work?

Doghouses.

_____

What's an upper class Puerto Rican home?

One where the ash trays don't have writing on them.

_____

Why does the Italian Army wear brown uniforms?

When they shit in their pants, it doesn't show.

_____

What did the Polack do when he went into the pay toilet and read the sign, "Don't Put Anything But Toilet Paper Into Toilet?"

He shit on the floor.

_____

Why do Polacks pick their noses with their fingers?

Because their tongues aren't long enough.

Did you hear about the Polish pirate?

He had a patch over both eyes.

_____

Did you hear about the black kid who actually put on a new pair of underwear everyday?

By Friday, he couldn't get his pants on.

_____

Did you hear about the famous Italian plastic surgeon?

He repairs Tupperware.

_____

Why haven't Polish astronomers made any important discoveries?

They refuse to work nights.

_____

Why aren't there very many black ventriloquists?

Even very few dummies will work for a nigger.

What do blacks call a dandelion in a pot?

The front lawn.

Why did the Polish scientist castrate himself?

He wanted to be eligible for the "No-Ball" Prize.

What did the Polack say when he saw his best friend on top of his wife?

"Down, Fido."

Why don't black kids have pet rocks?

They run away.

Why is a JAP like stale beer?

You'll get no head from either one.

What do they call pocketbooks in Poland?

Doggie bags.

Why do Polish children wear shoes?

To break them of the habit of biting their toenails.

At the Miss Universe contest, how do you identify Miss Poland?

She's the one who looks like she has a Brillo pad under each armpit.

Why did the Polack stand up with a piece of bread at the dinner table?

He wanted to propose a toast.

A Polack gets off the train with his face green as a lime. His friend asks, "What's wrong?"

"I had to ride backwards. Riding backwards makes me sick."

"Why didn't you change seats with the guy opposite you?" the friend asked.

"I couldn't," the Polack replied. "There wasn't anybody sitting there."

———————————

What's the easiest job in the world?

A mind reader in Poland.

———————————

What's a "lubber?"

A Japanese condom.

———————————

What's "plegnant?"

What Japanese girls get if their boyfriends don't use a lubber.

What did the Polack do after his cat was run over by a steamroller?

He stood there with a long puss.

———————————

How many Polacks does it take to screw in a light bulb?

If they can find one who can do it, they award him a Ph.D.

———————————

What did the Polish short order cook give his fiance?

A 21 carat onion ring.

———————————

How can you make an Irishman's tongue turn black?

Pour whiskey on a freshly-tarred road.

———————————

What did the Italian do when his wife complained about slack in the clothesline?

He moved his house.

Did you hear about the Polack who's wife asked him to change his baby son?

He showed up two hours later with a baby girl.

———————————

Did you hear about the black dude who signed an organ transplant agreement?

When he died, a baboon got his heart, an orangutan got his liver, and a gorilla got his eyes.

———————————

What's black and blue and floats down the river?

A white man who laughs at the last joke while waiting in line at Kentucky Fried Chicken.

———————————

Why did the Polack wear only one boot?

The weather forecast was for one foot of snow.

———————————

Did you hear about the fat Polack kid?

He was so big he could only play Seek.

How many blacks does it take to eat a rabbit dinner?

Three. One to eat and two to watch in each direction for cars.

_____

What's the name of the Puerto Rican national airline?

Air Pollution.

_____

What's the toughest thing about hiring a new black janitor?

Showing him how the wastebaskets work.

_____

Why did the Polish woman limp?

She cut her toes shaving.

_____

Did you hear about the Polish woman who was pondering a new hairdo?

She couldn't decide whether to have the hair on her legs braided or curled.

Why does it cost Polish women $25,000 to have a baby?

$2,000 in medical expenses, $23,000 to pay someone to sleep with them.

———————————

How does the newspaper report of a Puerto Rican social event read?

Among those wounded by gunshots were . . .

———————————

Why is it impossible to walk across New Jersey?

No one can hold his nose that long.

———————————

Why are there no active volcanos in Puerto Rico?

There are no virgins to sacrifice.

———————————

What do you call a '64 Chevy?

A Puerto Rican bridal suite.

What did they do in Poland when a manure silo fell over?

Called in troops to shoot the looters.

Did you hear about the Polack who was killed during a pie-eating contest?

The cow sat on him.

How can you tell Polacks from the other students?

Most students wear name tags; Polacks wear "Vacant" signs.

How ugly are Polish farm wives?

So ugly Polish cows give yogurt.

How does a Polack fan himself?

He holds his hands still and waves his face in front of it.

Why did they remove the speed bumps from Southern roads?

Because the blacks were doing their laundry on them.

———————————

Why were the Puerto Ricans pushing their building down the street?

They were trying to jump-start the furnace.

———————————

What do "The NFL Today" and the Miss Poland Contest have in common?

They're both pigskin previews.

———————————

Why are Eskimo hookers like congressmen?

They both are terrific at snow jobs.

———————————

What's the difference between yogurt and Poland?

Yogurt has culture.

Did you hear about the Polish terrorists?

They attacked the Special Olympics.

———————————

Why did the Italian girl get pregnant?

She fed her birth control pills to storks.

———————————

A man arrived at work to find his Polish friend laughing hysterically. "What's so funny?" he asked.

The Polack said, "I just found out that the foreman has been paying $20 to screw my wife."

"What's so funny about that?"

"That guy is crazy," the Polack said. "I screw her for free."

———————————

The gun went off and eight women dove into the pool for the Olympic 100 meter breaststroking heat. An American won in a little under two minutes, six other contestants finished within ten seconds of her—and the Polish girl came in 35 minutes later.

When she surfaced, impatient judges circled her. But before they could speak, the Polish girl shouted angrily, "I want to file a protest. Those other girls used their arms."

How do you wash genitals?

The same way you wash Jews.

Did you hear about the blind Polish prostitute?

You had to hand it to her.

Two Polacks were on a tour of the Florida Everglades. They were sitting on a dock eating sandwiches when one turned to the other and said, "Hey, an alligator just tore off my leg."

His shocked friend asked, "Which one?"

"I don't know," the first Polack replied. "All those gators look alike to me."

Did you hear about the Polack who cut correspondence school?

He sent in empty envelopes.

What has feathers and glows in the dark?

Chicken Kiev.

Who were the first two casualties of the Chernobyl disaster?

The two guys who told Gorbachov.

How bad was the radiation in Scandinavia?

Well, Swedish women are now giving birth to blue-haired, blonde-eyed babies.

How many Russians does it take to change a light bulb?

None—they all glow in the dark.

Why aren't Russian women upset about what's happening to their babies?

They've heard that two heads are better than one.

Are the citizens of Kiev angry about Chernobyl?

They're doing a slow burn.

What did they do with the Ukrainian wheat?

Sold it as self-baking bread.

How can you tell a woman's from Kiev?

She's simply radiant.

How do you identify a Ukrainian ranch?

The rats are as big as the cows.

Did you hear about the new great Russian novel?

AND BRIGHTLY FLOWS THE DON.

What's between Kiev and Stockholm?

The Glow-Bi Desert.

How do you catch fish from Lake Kiev?

Glow worms.

What do you call a Ukrainian sent to Siberia?

Lucky.

What's the latest weather report from Kiev?

Hazy, humid, with a high of 2000 degrees.

Why aren't there any more barges on Russian rivers?

They've been eaten by the 2 ton bass.

What are the Russians doing with the Chernobyl nuclear power plant?

They turned it into a synagogue.

_____

What do you call Communists from Kiev?

Baldchiviks.

_____

Why are the people from Kiev like a popular alcoholic beverage?

They're both Black Russians.

_____

What do Ethiopian parents do for their child's first birthday?

Put a flower on his grave.

_____

What do Ethiopian women call oral sex?

Dinner.

Why are Ethiopians so gullible?

They'll swallow anything.

———————————

What's black and full of cobwebs?

An Ethiopian's asshole.

———————————

What do you call an Ethiopian with a dime on his head?

A nail.

———————————

How many Ethiopians can you get in a telephone booth?

All of them.

———————————

Why do Ethiopian fathers jerk off three times a day?

They have to feed the baby.

What's the most useless present you can buy an Ethiopian?

A toothbrush.

What's the second most useless present?

After dinner mints.

What's the most useless article of clothing?

A dinner jacket.

What do you call an Ethiopian with his legs apart?

A wishbone.

Where do Ethiopian children shop?

Flies-R-Us.

Why are Ethiopian mothers like McDonald's?

They both turn out quarter-pounders.

What's 6-12-6?

The measurements of Miss Ethiopia.

A Polack was sitting on the porch with his girl friend when a pigeon flew overhead and deposited a load on her arm.

The girl turned to the Polack and said, "Go in the house and get me some toilet paper."

"Why bother?" the Polack replied. "That bird's a mile away by now."

How can you tell a Polish secretary?

Her computer screen is covered with Wite-Out.

Did you hear Mayor Koch pledged to improve transportation in Harlem?

He's going to plant the trees closer together.

What's Mayor Koch's solution to overcrowding in Harlem?

He's persuaded Union Carbide to build a plant there.

———————————

Why did General Motors recall their new Cadillacs?

Watermelons wouldn't fit in the glove compartment.

———————————

Why is there so little Puerto Rican literature?

Spray paint only went on the market twenty years ago.

———————————

Did you hear about the Polack who wanted to take a day off?

He called in dead.

———————————

Why did the Polack lose his contact lens?

The putty fell out of his eye.

What did the valley girl say while she was giving head to a black?

"Gag me with a coon!"

Why did they kick the Polack out of the wedding reception?

He tried to flush the punch bowl.

Why are Puerto Ricans great laxatives?

They irritate the shit out of everybody.

What did the Polack do when he thought his wife was cheating on him?

Dusted her for fingerprints.

Why do black kids have such foul mouths?

You ever see a black home with soap?

What's a shit?

A Greek's wet dream.

_____

Why don't they let Polish women swim in the ocean?

The tuna get hard-ons.

Chapter Two:

DOUBLY GROSS CELEBRITY JOKES

Why wasn't anyone surprised Reagan got nose cancer after his operation?

He's always had his head up his ass.

Why was Pia Zadora voted celebrity of the year by the American Medical Association?

Because her movies make people sick.

What kind of bath toy did Joan Crawford buy her kids?

A toaster.

How did Joan Crawford cure her children of bed wetting?

She bought them an electric blanket.

What's the first thing a Hollywood starlet does every morning?

Gets up and drives home.

Did you hear about the starlet who suffers from sex insomnia?

She can't keep her thighs closed.

Why doesn't Rock Hudson know how he got AIDS?

He doesn't have eyes in the back of his head.

Why did Rock Hudson's diet give him AIDS?

He ate the wrong kind of fruits.

Why is Ralph Nader so humorless?

He can't recall jokes.

———————

Why did the little girl blow Frosty the Snowman?

She loved ice cream.

———————

Why did Liz Taylor go on a diet?

She looked in a mirror and saw double shins.

———————

Why hasn't the starlet visited Mt. Rushmore?

She can't decide which face to sit on.

———————

Did you hear that President Reagan asked Rock Hudson to go to Ethiopia to help relieve starvation?

His trip is called "Live AIDS."

Why did the starlet turn down a lucrative series offer from NBC?

She wanted nothing to do with a "peacock."

_____

What's unique about the starlet's anatomy?

She has no private parts.

_____

How can you tell Pia Zadora's baby in the nursery?

It's the one in the see-through diapers.

_____

When did Arnold Schwarzeneger realize he was getting a little over-developed?

When he found out he was giving Dolly Parton an inferiority complex.

_____

What do you get when you cross Conan the Barbarian with Mr. T?

Arnold Schwarze-Nigger.

What's "mine shaft?"

What Arnold Schwarzeneger calls his penis.

―――――――――――――

Did you hear about the new airline for senior citizens started by Bob Hope and George Burns?

It's called "Incontinental."

―――――――――――――

Why did President Reagan approve a $10 million grant to study "Webster?"

He wants to find a way to keep all little nigger kids that size.

―――――――――――――

Why did George Burns cancel a concert date?

Something unexpected came up.
What did his girl friend say?

"Oh, God!"

What's the difference between the starlet and the Queen Mary?

It takes a few tugs to get the Queen Mary out of her slip.

_____

Did you hear about the Hollywood star who did the pilot for a half-hour sit-com?

It's called "I Love Loosely."

_____

Why did Joan Crawford often take a clothes hanger to her kids?

Because she was angry she forgot to use it on them before they were born.

_____

How does Clint Eastwood like his women?

Dirty, hairy.

_____

Who was the eighth dwarf who got kicked out for sitting on Snow White's face?

Sleazy.

What's Dean Martin's favorite drink?

The next one.

Did you hear that William Holden died from a form of nervous breakdown?

Bottle fatigue.

Why did Joan Crawford always come home drunk and leave her clothes on the floor?

She was in them.

Why did Madonna call her album "Like A Virgin?"

It was an inside joke.

Why doesn't Dolly Parton make topless movies?

They'd flop.

What did Bob Hope sing after Dolly Parton was on his show?

"Thanks for the mammaries."

———————————

Who legalized marijuana?

A joint session of Congress.

———————————

Why is Madonna like a popular breakfast treat?

They're both pop tarts.

———————————

Is Madonna literate?

Well, she often takes Penn in hand.

———————————

Why is Dolly Parton the luckiest woman in the world?

Her cup runneth over.

Did you hear that the Republicans have issued toilet paper with Ronald Reagan's picture on every sheet?

That's so the assholes can see who they voted for.

———————————

What do you call a speech by Mohammud Ali?

Racial slurs.

———————————

What's a Ronald Reagan Sandwich?

One that's so full of baloney you can't swallow it.

———————————

What's the caption on a picture of Jimmy Carter, Jerry Ford, and Richard Nixon?

"See no evil, hear no evil, and evil."

———————————

What do Boy George and the Boy Scouts have in common?

They both think camping is great fun.

Why does Martina Navratilova spend so much time in Europe?

She misses her native tongue.

_____

How do we know exactly how and when Elvis Presley died in the john?

He left a log.

_____

What did the talent scout say about Dolly Parton?

"She's got a great future ahead of her."

_____

What did the doctors say as they transferred Mohammud Ali from one ward to another?

"Pass the squash."

_____

What was unique about presidents Washington and Jefferson?

They were the last two white men to have those names.

What happened to Renee Richards' penis?

It was snatched.

_____

Why did it take Renee Richards time to recover from her sex change operation?

She woke up dis-jointed.

_____

Why was Renee Richards lonely after her operation?

She was rootless.

_____

Why won't Renee Richards let her doctor take blood samples?

She doesn't want another prick.

_____

Why isn't there a Renee Richards Fan Club?

She lost her only member.

Where do Elvis Presley, John Belushi, Natalie Wood, and Grace Kelly vacation?

Club Dead.

_____

If Elvis Presley were on stage today, how would he do?

He'd stink.

_____

Why can't Boy George tell dirty jokes?

Even when he's alone, he's in mixed company.

_____

What's James Brady's position at the White House?

Pet secretary.

_____

What's gibberish?

A conversation between James Brady and Mohammud Ali.

Why did Johnny and Joanna Carson separate?

Joanna starred in the "not-tonight" show.

What happened when Joanna Carson heard about the famine in Ethiopia?

She was so upset she went out and spent $10,000 on clothes.

Why is it unlikely Ted Kennedy, Jr. will ever be President?

All the other candidates have a leg up on him.

Why did Ted Kennedy, Jr. take off his artificial leg?

He wanted to stump for his father.

Why doesn't Boy George marry Marilyn?

They can't decide who'll wear the wedding dress.

What did Parkinson's Disease give Howard Cosell that he never gave anyone else?

A fair shake.

_____

What do you get when you cross Boy George and a New York Yankee?

Ball Boy George.

_____

How chic is Jacqueline Onassis?

Tres chic. Even her period is French Provencial.

_____

What was the one consolation for Jackie the day after John Kennedy was assassinated?

Some of his brains finally rubbed off on her.

_____

Why aren't there any new John Lennon songs?

These days, John's de-composing.

Did you hear about the couple who named their son after Howard Cosell?

He's called "Palsy."

What do you call Howard Cosell these days?

Motor-disease mouth.

Is it unfair that people call Princess Anne a horse?

Well, her gynecologist is a vet.

What's Roman Polanski's motto?.

"Spare the rod, spoil the child."

Why is Roman Polanski leaving his estate in trust for his girl friend?

He doesn't want her to touch it until she's thirteen.

Did you hear that Roman Polanski is dating a teenager?

Yes, but she's got the body of an eight-year-old.

What does Reagan plan to do if the Democrats nominate Ted Kennedy in 1988?

Pardon Sirhan Sirhan.

Why doesn't Princess Anne have to carry an American Express Card?

Her number is tatooed inside her lip.

Why is Princess Anne's interest in nature amazing?

Well, considering what it did to her . . .

Why is Queen Elizabeth so popular in India?

Hindus worship the cow.

Did you hear that Queen Elizabeth grew up thinking sex was evil?

And when Princess Anne was born, she had her proof.

Why has Joan Rivers never performed in Poland?

There's no one worth shitting on over there.

Who did they call in when William Schroeder had a stroke?

Mr. Goodwrench.

What do the nurses do when William Schroeder gets cranky?

Step on his hose until he behaves.

Did you hear William Schroeder had another heart transplant?

The donor was C3PO.

Why did the hostess ask Claus Von Bulow to come to dinner without his wife?

She wasn't serving vegetables.

Did you hear about the new Vanessa Williams scandal?

They found nude pictures of her parents in National Geographic.

What do most Americans feel about the way Reagan has handled the country's finances?

They've never been more indebted.

Why did Ronald Reagan scream out in bed the other night?

After six years, he finally achieved single-digit inflation.

Why is George Wallace the most honest politician alive?

He's always called a spade a spade.

Why does masturbating make Superman stronger?

Because he's pumping iron.

———————————

How did Ma and Pa Kent know Clark was wetting his bed?

There was rust on the sheets.

———————————

Why will Lois Lane never be anemic?

Because of all the iron injections she gets from Superman.

———————————

Why do they call Ronald Reagan the "prophylactic" President?

Because he gives you the feeling of safety while you're being screwed.

———————————

Do Ronald and Nancy Reagan have any problems in bed?

Not as long as they use Rustoleum instead of vasoline.

Why was it a mistake to elect a man of Reagan's age?

Because he's making the country baroque.

_____

How many White House aides does it take to change a light bulb?

None. They prefer to leave Reagan in the dark.

_____

Why did the Democrats hire Jane Wyman?

Because she knows how to screw Ronald Reagan and dump him.

_____

What's Ronald Reagan's idea of happy hour?

His afternoon nap.

_____

Is Mary Lou Retton still a virgin?

Yes, but her coach is working hard on her vault.

What did Ronald Reagan think when he heard millions were starving in Africa?

He thought it was a good start.

––––––––––––––––

Why is Dolly Parton insanely jealous of Miss Lillian Carter?

Miss Lillian had the two biggest boobs in the world—Jimmy and Billy.

––––––––––––––––

How can you tell Richard Nixon's been walking on the beach?

He only leaves heel marks.

––––––––––––––––

Why did Richard Nixon cancel his plans to add his bust to Mount Rushmore?

The Army Corps of Engineers told him there wasn't room for two more faces.

How does Richard Nixon know the country's beginning to forget Watergate?

When people wave at him these days, some use all five fingers.

———————————

What's Claus Von Bulow's favorite song?

"When Sonny Gets Blue."

Chapter Three:

DOUBLY GROSS ANIMAL JOKES

How do you tell a Scottish stag party?

A sheep jumps out of the cake.

_____

Which comes first, the chicken or the egg?

Neither. It's the rooster who comes.

_____

How do crabs leave the hospital?

On crotches.

_____

What do you call a Scottish ladies' man?

A shepherd.

What's the leading major at Scottish Universities?

Animal husbandry.

How do you seduce a Scotsman?

Look at him sheepishly.

Why did the veterinarian's wife divorce him?

Instead of screwing her, he liked to bury himself in his work.

Why don't chickens wear underwear?

Because their peckers are on their faces.

If storks bring babies, what bird doesn't?

Swallows.

What's the best way to stop the stork from coming?

Shoot into the air.

If small eggs sell for $1.00 a dozen and large eggs sell for $1.25 a dozen, what kind does a smart chicken lay?

Small eggs. Who wants to bust their ass for a lousy quarter?

Why do Scottish men love sheep?

After you fuck them, you can eat them.

Why did the farm boy stop screwing the cow?

It was too far around to kiss her.

What's the difference between kinky and perverted?

Kinky is using a feather; perverted is using the whole chicken.

How can you tell if a Scotsman is into S&M?

He keeps his sheep on a leash.

———————————

On what grounds did Mickey Mouse divorce Minnie?

Insanity. She was fucking Goofy.

———————————

Why did Kermit hesitate to marry Miss Piggy?

Her family's a bunch of awful boars.

———————————

Why is Kermit the Frog like a rock musician?

They're both into fucking pigs.

———————————

What's the difference between a fly and a mosquito?

You can't sew a zipper on a mosquito.

What sound does Kermit make when he gets horny?

Rub-it . . . rub-it . . . rub-it . . .

What kind of bath oil did Kermit buy Miss Piggy?

Hogwash.

An alligator gets out of a cab at the airport. A redcap asks him, "Carry your bag, sir?"

"Sure," the alligator says. "But be careful—that's my wife."

What do you get when you cross a gorilla and a mink?

A fur coat whose sleeves are too long.

What has a hundred balls and fucks rabbits?

A shotgun.

What do you get when you cross an eel and a cucumber?

I don't know, but there's 50 old maids waiting in line to buy one.

———————————

What do you get when you cross a chicken and a hooker?

A chicken that lays you.

———————————

What did Miss Piggy say when the phone rang unexpectedly?

"I can't talk now. I've got a frog in my throat."

———————————

Why does Miss Piggy talk funny?

She has warts on her lips.

———————————

What did the termite say when he walked into the pub?

"Is the bar tender here?"

How do you know it's really cold out?

When your dog sticks to the fire hydrant.

―――――――――

What venereal disease do rabbits get?

V.W.

―――――――――

What do you call a cow with no legs?

Beef on the hoof.

―――――――――

What goes "hoppity . . . click . . . hoppity . . . click?"

The Easter bunny with polio.

―――――――――

What do you call a rabbit with AIDS?

Peter Rotten Tail.

What do you do with a dog with no legs?

Take it for a spin.

How can you tell a politician is a pervert?

When his campaign promise is "A chicken in every bed."

Chapter Four:

DOUBLY GROSS
HOMOSEXUAL JOKES

Why haven't scientists discovered a cure for AIDS?

Because they can't teach laboratory rats to butt-fuck.

———————————

What do gays think of anal sex?

It hurts at first, but then it's fun in the end.

———————————

How do you tell which house belongs to the fairy?

The door mat reads, "Wipe your knees."

———————————

What's invisible and smells like cum?

Faggot farts.

How do you make a fruit punch?

Goose him.

———————————

How can you tell San Francisco Mounted Police?

They ride sidesaddle.

———————————

What's the most fun in going to a macho gay bar?

Going in the back room for the cock fighting.

———————————

Why is AIDS like vitamin C?

You get both from drinking fruit juice.

———————————

Why do war chiefs always put gay Indians in front when they attack?

Because they're brave suckers.

What's AIDS?

The ultimate diet aid.

If horse racing is the Sport of Kings, what's the Sport of Queens?

Drag racing.

What happens to guys who spend the night in a gay bar?

They wake up with a queer taste in their mouths.

Why can't faggots play the outfield?

They drop every fly they get under.

What's a lesbian?

A pansy without a stem.

Why did the gay cover himself from head to toe with whipped cream before he went to the costume party?

He was going as a wet dream.

———————————

Why is a fag at an orgy like a turkey?

Because he'll gobble, gobble, gobble, until you cut off his head.

———————————

Why is heterosexual sperm fresher than gay sperm?

Most gay sperm comes in a can.

———————————

What's the difference between California and Florida?

In California, the fruits pick you.

———————————

What's the difference between a bull dyke and a bull?

Five pounds and a flannel shirt.

Why do very few gay men play the flute?

They're always forgetting to blow instead of suck.

————————

Why did the fag strip naked and tie a string to his dick?

He was going to a costume party as a pull toy.

————————

What's the most popular card game in gay bars?

Pansy poker—Queens are wild and no straights are allowed.

————————

What's the difference between herpes and AIDS?

Herpes is a love story. AIDS is a fairy tale.

————————

Why has there never been a Hurricane Bruce?

The Weather Bureau's waiting for a hurricane that never stops blowing.

Did you hear about the horrible new disease that's transmitted by lesbian sex?

It's called MAIDS.

———————————

What's a gay's definition of a lousy party?

One where there's ten guys to every man.

———————————

Why are homosexual novels so predictable?

The hero always gets his man in the end.

———————————

What do fags eat in the summer?

Spermsickles.

———————————

What's the difference between a sodomist and a suppository?

None.

What do you call gays who are into S&M?

Suckers for punishment.

———————————

Why are male hairdressers such pricks?

You are what you eat.

———————————

The friends of the very gay man were surprised when he married a young girl and totally astounded when she became pregnant. One day two friends met the flaming fag by the beach. Noticing the wife's obvious condition, they asked, "How in the hell did that happen?"

The fag pointed to a tall, muscular blond hunk standing next to his wife. "It's all due to that marvelous young man."

"Is he your wife's lover?" the friend asked.

"Not exactly," said the fag with a big grin. "He's our go-between."

———————————

Why did Congress abolish the job of page?

Pages were the objects of too many Congressional probes.

Why did the San Francisco Police Department fire all its gay detectives?

They blew nearly every case.

_____

What does AIDS stand for?

"Adios, Infected Dick Sucker."

_____

What's a gay Western?

A movie in which all the good guys are hung.

_____

Who did the gay guy hire to find out who gave him AIDS?

Dick Tracer.

_____

What can you get from a Mexican fag?

Foreign AIDS.

What's the worst part about having AIDS?

When your friends have an orgy, you can't cum.

What's Ronald Reagan's solution to the cost of welfare?

AIDS for dependent children.

What's worse than your doctor telling you you have AIDS?

Your mother telling you.

Why are your chances of getting AIDS like good manners?

Both depend on how you've been reared.

Why did the gay shepherd go broke?

His herd died of AIDS.

Why is an AIDS victim's prick like an M-16?

They're both deadly weapons.

_____

What do you call four rough-and-tough fags in a custom van?

The AIDS team.

_____

What do they call homosexuals in the Army?

AIDS-de-camp.

_____

Why did the fag storm out of the fast food restaurant?

He found out Big Mac was a hamburger.

_____

What did one gay sperm say to the other?

"How am I supposed to find the egg in all this shit?"

Violence seemed about to erupt as the crowd in the bar outside the military base argued about whether sailors or Marines had bigger pricks. To settle the issue, the bartender suggested that the sailors lay out their pieces on one long table and the Marines on another long table.

Both sides agreed, and the display was completed, just as two fags walked into the bar. One looked at the tables, turned to his friend and squealed with delight. "Look, Bruce—it's a buffet!"

———————

What song did the fags play for their friends who have AIDS?

Taps.

———————

Why do they call AIDS a social disease?

It produces a lot of lonely assholes.

———————

Why do gays continue to have sex despite the risk of AIDS?

Because they're born suckers.

Why did Prince Philip stop screwing his wife?

Because he read you got AIDS from queens.

Why are they shooting the new movie about Ethiopia in San Francisco?

They're casting AIDS victims in the leading roles.

How do you describe a gay's life?

Asses to ashes.

What's the hottest new product in Greenwich Village?

Designer urns.

What do lesbians send their lovers on Valentine's Day?

A bouquet of batteries.

Why is AIDS like supper on the farm?

You come and get it.

Chapter Five:

DOUBLY GROSS CRIPPLE JOKES

A guy picked up a blonde at a bar, and after having a few drinks, they went to a hotel room. When the blonde got undressed, the guy was astounded to see her unstrapping a wooden leg. He was so drunk and horny, however, that he went ahead and screwed her.

Later, when the blonde fell asleep, the guy began fiddling with the artificial leg. Finally, he found he'd taken it apart and he couldn't get it back together. He went out in the hall and stopped a man who reeked of booze. "Can you help me?" he asked. "I've got a woman in my room with one leg apart and I can't get it back together."

"Hell," the drunk replied. "I've got a woman in my room with two legs apart, and I can't even find the fucking room."

How do lepers commit sexual suicide?

By giving head.

Why did the boy cut off his mother's leg?

He wanted to stump her just once.

———————————

Why aren't lepers sexually spontaneous?

If they rip off a piece, they can't put it back.

———————————

Why don't lepers make good executives?

They go to pieces under pressure.

———————————

Why was the leper hooker limping around on one leg?

When she didn't get any customers, she took 25% off.

———————————

Why do lepers make good wives?

If they give you lip once, it will be the last time.

How do you stop a leper from robbing banks?

Dis-arm him.

———————

Why did they stop the leper football game?

There was a handoff at the line of scrimmage.

———————

Why did they stop the leper baseball game?

The left fielder dropped a ball.

———————

How do I know lepers won't read this book?

They're afraid of laughing their asses off.

———————

What do you call a guy with no arms and no legs with graffitti on him?

Wally.

What do you call a guy with no arms and no legs who's upside down in the end zone?

Spike.

―――――――――――

What do you call a Spanish guy with no arms and no legs who's very pale?

Juan.

―――――――――――

What do you call a guy with no arms and no legs who's rude?

Kurt.

―――――――――――

What do you call a guy with no arms and no legs who's halfway down Tina Turner's throat?

Mike.

―――――――――――

What do you call a guy with no arms and no legs who's been left out in the grass all night?

Dewey.

Why shouldn't you ever marry a woman with no hands?

You'll never know how she feels.

_____

What do you call a woman with no arms, no legs, and no torso?

Muffy.

_____

What do you call a woman with no arms and no legs who spreads for bread?

Marge.

_____

What do you call a guy with no arms and no legs who sells drugs?

Rich.

_____

What do you call a guy who's pretending to have no arms and no legs?

Josh.

What do you call a woman with no arms and no legs who's caught on the fence?

Barb.

_____

What do you call a woman with no arms and no legs who's surrounded by truckers?

Dinah.

_____

What do you call a guy with no arms and no legs who's an impotent lover?

Dud.

_____

What do you call a guy who's pretending to have no arms and no legs for money?

Con.

_____

What do you call a woman with no arms and no legs who loves oral sex?

Heddy.

What do you call a woman who has no arms and no legs every four weeks?

Flo.

_____

What do you call a woman with no arms and no legs with a weak bladder?

Pia.

_____

What do you call a woman with no arms and no legs who's been force fed beans?

Gail.

_____

What do you do when an epileptic has a fit in your swimming pool?

Throw in a box of Tide and your laundry.

_____

Why are lepers so obnoxious?

They're always giving you a piece of their mind.

Why did the brothel in the leper colony close?

The tips weren't worth it.

———————

What happened to the leper who went to New York?

Someone stole his kneecaps.

———————

How do you know a leper has been in your shower?

Your bar of soap has grown.

———————

Why did the leper go back into the bathroom?

He left his Head and Shoulders in the shower.

———————

What do they serve cannibals who are late for dinner?

Cold shoulders.

Chapter Six:

DOUBLY GROSS JUVENILE
AND CANNIBAL JOKES

Because her students were getting tired of show and tell, the teacher decided to have the children come to the front of the room to describe any unusual hobbies their parents had.

First was a little girl, who said, "My mother has a collection of antique dolls."

"Very good," the teacher said. "And you, Harold."

Harold said, "My father is the champion golfer at his country club."

"Very good. Freddy?"

Freddy announced that his mother's roses won a prize at the Garden club. The teacher nodded her approval, then called on Sally.

She stood, but didn't say a word until the teacher said, "Don't your parents do anything you can tell us about?"

Sally thought, then said, "About all I know is that my father eats light bulbs."

"My word!" the teacher exclaimed. "Are you sure?"

Sally nodded. "I was passing their bedroom the other night when I heard my father say, 'If you turn out the light, honey, I'll eat it.'"

A young boy accompanied his father to a horse auction. He watched his father enter a stall, bend down, and run his hands up and down the animal's legs.

"What are you doing, Dad?" the boy asked.

"This is the way you decide whether or not to buy a horse," his father replied.

The boy's face grew serious. "Gee, Dad, we better hurry home. The milk man stopped in yesterday, and I think he wants to buy Mommy."

———————

The eight-year-old kid swaggered into the lounge and demanded of the barmaid, "Give me a double Scotch on the rocks."

"What do you want to do, get me in trouble?" the barmaid asked.

"Maybe later," the kid said. "Right now, I just want the Scotch."

———————

When do cannibals leave the table?

When everyone's eaten.

The drought had lasted two years, and the African tribe was beginning to suffer. The tribal council convened a meeting.

No solution was offered until a young tribal member said, "I know what to do."

The elders scoffed, but the chief asked him to explain his plan.

"It's simple," the young man said. "We send a letter to the Russian embassy telling them we're having trouble with our crops. They'll send us seed, equipment, and 100 technicians. Then we'll let the Americans know what the Russians are doing, and they'll send seed, equipment, and 100 more technicians."

"That won't do any good," one elder complained. "All the seed in the world won't do us any good in the drought."

"I know," the young man said. "But we'll just eat the technicians."

———————

Why did the cannibal roast the fortune teller for hours?

He liked his mediums well-done.

———————

What do cannibals put out at cocktail parties instead of hor d'oeuvres?

Finger bowls.

103

"Mommy, Mommy, why can't we bury the baby?"

"Shut up and keep flushing."

———————————

Little Joey's father lost his job, and the conversation around the dinner table increasingly revolved around money. By the end of the first month, Joey's mother spent most of the day wondering how in the hell they'd pay the mortgage.

The next day, Joey packs a bag and runs away from home. He gets as far as the bus station, when a cop stops him and asks him why he's running away.

"My parents are afraid they're going to lose the house. Then last night, I walked by the bedroom and heard my Pop yell, "I'm pulling out." Then Ma shouted, "I'm coming, too."

"So?" the cop said.

"Well," Joey went on, "I ain't about to stick around and get stuck with the fucking mortgage."

———————————

"Mommy, Mommy, why are we out in this boat?"

"Shut up and tie the concrete blocks back on your feet."

"Mommy, Mommy, why can't we get a garbage disposal?"

"Shut up and keep chewing."

"Mommy, Mommy, why can't I breathe?"

"Good, it's working."

What's the definition of trust?

Two cannibals having 69.

"Mommy, Mommy, why do I have so many warts."

"Because you're a toad, that's why."

"Mommy, Mommy, I can't stop bleeding."

"Shut up, you knew there was barbed wire on the staircase."

"Mommy, Mommy, can I cut little sister's hair."

"No. Run right downstairs and put her head back in the coffin."

———————————

"Mommy, Mommy, why is Daddy running so fast?"

"Shut up and reload."

———————————

The teacher had been after her sixth graders to bring in their five dollars for the class picture. Dismayed at their tardiness, one day she got up in front of the class and said, "Class, think how much you're going to treasure this picture twenty-five years from now. You'll pull it out and say, 'There's my friend, Jane, she's a lawyer now; there's my friend, Billy, he's a Congressman . . .'"

Suddenly, a voice from the back of the room interrupted, "There's my teacher, she's dead."

———————————

The luscious young blonde was just out of school and in her first fifth grade teaching job. The first day she got up on a ladder to write something at the top of the blackboard. She heard one of her students laugh, then turned and demanded, "Leon, what's so funny?"

"I can see up your skirt," the boy said.

She turned red. "That's very naughty. You're suspended for two days."

The next day the teacher bent over to pick up a book, only to hear another boy laugh. When asked what was so funny, Freddie said, "Teacher, I can see your thighs."

"You naughty boy," the teacher said, "you're suspended for 10 days."

That night, the teacher had a heavy date, and came to school without putting on her panties. She assigned the class to do some math exercises, then sat down in her chair. She dozed off, only to wake when yet another boy laughed.

"What's so funny, Johnny?" she demanded.

"Well, your legs were wide open when you fell asleep," Johnny said as he got to his feet. "So I guess my school days are over."

One cannibal went up to another and said, "You look awful. What's wrong?"

"I had that missionary for lunch," the second cannibal said. "And ever since I've been burping and belching."

"You should know better than to eat a missionary," the first cannibal said. "You just can't keep a good man down."

A father came home from a long business trip to find his son riding a very fancy new 10 speed bike. "Where did you get the money for that bike? It must have cost $300."

"Easy, Dad," the boy replied. "I earned it hiking."

"Come on," the father said. "Tell me the truth."

"That is the truth," the boy said. "Every night you were gone, Mr. Reynolds from the grocery store would come over to see Mom. He'd give me a $20 bill and tell me to take a hike."

How many babysitters does it take to change a light bulb?

None. They don't make Huggies small enough.

Why did the cannibals check the dental records at the Home for Brain-Damaged Children?

They wanted to know which vegetables they were eating.

What did the cannibal give his wife on Valentine's Day?

A box of Farmer's Fannies.

One cannibal stopped into another's hut and was surprised to see a large new refrigerator.

"Gee, that's terrific," the first cannibal said. "How much does it hold?"

"I'm not exactly sure," the second cannibal replied. "But it was big enough for the two men who delivered it."

———————————

A young cannibal girl went to Club Med for vacation. When she got back, she told her girlfriends about this handsome young man she met on the beach.

"You're kidding," one of her friends said. "No man could be that good."

"I'll prove it to you," the cannibal girl said. "I've got what's left of him in my suitcase."

———————————

When do cannibals get depressed?

When they're fed up with people.

The teacher returned from the principal's office to see all of her students in the back of the room, cheering. She rushed through the crowd and found little Johnny and Mary naked. Johnny was on top, pumping away.

The teacher grabbed Johnny roughly and demanded, "Just what do you think you're doing?"

"What you said, teacher," Johnny replied.

"You told us to practice multiplying. I was the only one who knew how, so I was showing the rest of them."

————————

The cannibal asked his wife, "What's for dinner?"

"Two old maids," she replied.

"Ugh," the cannibal grunted. "Leftovers again."

————————

The mother walked into the freezing living room to see her son sitting in front of the dying fire.

"Why haven't you poked the fire?" she asked her son.

"On account of Fuzzy, our kitten."

"What does Fuzzy have to do with it?" the mother asked.

"A little while ago Fuzzy fell into the fireplace and burned up," the boy replied. "And I just don't have the heart to poke her ashes."

A woman visiting a friend's house walks into the little boy's room. He's sitting on the floor, staring into a jar full of butterflies. "What are you doing?" she asks.

"Collecting butterflies is my hobby," little Johnny replies. "I caught these today."

"That's nice," the lady says. "But I have to tell you something. If you don't punch holes in the top of the jar, your butterflies will suffocate and die."

Little Johnny shrugs. "Who cares? It's only a hobby."

––––––––––––

Little five year old Tommy went with his mother when she took the new baby to the pediatrician. While they were waiting, the nurse was playing with the baby and saying, "Gee, I wish I had a cute little baby like you."

"You could have," Tommy piped up. "You just have to stay home and fuck every night like my Mom and Dad."

––––––––––––

How do you know you've bought illegitimate Rice Krispies?

They've got snap, crackle—but no pop.

Chapter Seven:

DOUBLY GROSS RELIGIOUS JOKES

Why were Moses' parents so lucky?

They not only had fun in bed, but they also made a prophet.

_____

If a dried grape is a raisin and a dried plum is a prune, what's dried cherry?

A nun.

The obviously pregnant young nun was called in front of the Mother Superior. "Can you explain how you allowed this to happen?" the Mother Superior angrily demanded.

"I went to Father Warren to confess my sins," the young nun explained. "I didn't want to let him touch me, but then he showed me where it was written right into the Scripture."

"I don't know any place in the Holy Bible where such outrageous conduct is condoned," the Mother Superior said.

"Right here," the nun said, opening the book. "It reads, 'Thy rod and Thy staff shall comfort me . . .'"

———————

When did the naive farm girl leave the convent?

When she found out "nun" really meant none.

———————

How did Jonah get out of the belly of the whale?

He ran around in circles until he was pooped.

Did you hear about the time Jesus walked into the Hilton Hotel?

He handed the clerk three nails and asked to be put up for the night.

How do we know the Pope is a drunk?

He's always talking about being drawn to the pure in spirits.

What do Mother Teresa and 7-Up have in common?

"Never had it, never will."

What do you get when you cross a hooker and Mother Teresa?

The black hole of Calcutta.

What's black and red and white and wrinkled and can' get through the door?

Mother Teresa with a spear through her head.

What's another name for the rhythm method of birth control?

Catholic roulette.

A very quiet, humble young nun was tragically killed in an auto accident. When she got to the pearly gates, however, St. Peter said, "Sister Marie, I've got some bad news and some good news. The bad news is that your room isn't ready yet. The good news is that, because you've been so devout, we're sending you to the French Riviera for a couple weeks to relax before you come back."

After a week, Sister Marie picked up the phone to hear St. Peter tell her there was still a delay. Sister Marie, after a moment's hesitation, said, "St. Peter, I have a confession to make. I smoked a cigarette."

"That's alright," St. Peter said. "We can forgive you."

A week later, the room still wasn't ready. This time, Sister Marie said, "St. Peter, I have another confession. I've had a glass of wine."

St. Peter smiled. "We can forgive you."

Two more weeks passed until the room was ready. St. Peter called Sister Marie, but the phone was off the hook. Worried, he went down to earth. He walked into the hotel room to find Sister Marie sprawled naked on the bed, alternately sucking on a bottle of whiskey and the cock of a young lifeguard.

She spotted the saint and called out, "Fuck heaven and hop on. After all those years in the convent, I could use another Peter."

———————————

One day St. Peter came down with a bad cold, so Christ gave him the day off and decided to man the gates of heaven himself. The morning was very slow until an old man came trudging slowly up the path to the pearly gates. When he arrived, Christ asked, "What have you done to deserve eternal reward?"

"I have led a simple life," the man replied. "I am just a humble carpenter. The only remarkable thing about my life was my son."

"Your son?"

"Yes," the carpenter replied. "He had a very unusual birth and went through a great transformation. Later he became renowned throughout the world, and he is remembered in men's hearts to this day."

As Christ listened to the story, tears formed in his eyes. He reached out, embraced the man tightly, then said, "Father, it's you."

The old man looked at him for a moment, then asked, "Pinocchio?"

A young female gymnast went to confession one morning right after practice. She was so happy after receiving absolution that she came out of the confessional, took a running start down the aisle, then did a series of back flips.

Mrs. O'Malley, who was waiting in the confession line, turned to her friend and said, "Glory be, would you look what Father Shannon is giving for penance today. And of all days for me not to be wearing my panties!"

———————————

One night after his evening service, a priest decided to take a walk. A wrong turn led him into the red light district. On the first corner, he saw a hooker dressed in a halter and hot pants leaning against a lamp post. Seeing the fallen woman, the priest went up and said, "My dear, I have spent my nights praying for you."

"No need to do that, Father," the hooker said. "I'm here every night. You can have me any time you want."

Chapter Eight:

DOUBLY GROSS
SENIOR CITIZEN JOKES

Two old men are sitting on a park bench on Main Street, shooting the breeze. One brags to the other, "You know that cute widow lady, Mrs. Durant? Well, I put it to her twice last night."

The other old man winced. "Golly, gee, George. I don't know how you do it. I haven't been able to get it up for five years."

"I have a secret," George said. "All you have to do is eat one of those loaves of Italian bread. I guarantee you, you'll be a new man."

Excitedly, his friend rushes to the bakery. He stands at the counter and tells the girl, "I want a dozen loaves of Italian bread."

"Are you sure?" the girl asked. "I warn you, it'll be hard before you finish the first loaf."

"God damn it!" the old man swears. "If everyone knows about Italian bread, why didn't someone tell me years ago?"

Why are old men like bumper stickers?

They're both hard to get off.

———————————

Two dapper old men sit on the porch of the retirement home every single afternoon. Two marriage-minded old ladies who move to the home set their sights on these most eligible of bachelors. The first day, they dress up in their finest evening gowns and parade past the porch three times. The men don't even look up.

Every day for two weeks, the old ladies try something new to get their attention—new hats, new hairdos, new jewelry. But the men don't give them a second glance.

Finally, the old ladies are so fed up one says to the other, "the only thing that's going to get the attention of those old coots is a little flesh."

The next afternoon, both ladies take off all their clothes in the bushes, then streak by the porch. One of the old men says to the other, "My God, what did they have on today?"

The other codger shakes his head. "Can't say for sure. But whatever they were wearing, it certainly needs ironing very badly."

Two old ladies were sitting on a park bench complaining about their husbands. "My husband's losing his mind," one lady said. "Last week he went out and spent $400 for a waterbed."

"That sounds exciting," the other lady said.

"Exciting, hell," the first old lady said. "The way my husband's thing has been reacting the last few years, that waterbed might as well be the Dead Sea."

———————————

A very wealthy old spinster had been pampered for years by her niece. She was distressed when the niece finally got married, and was put further out of sorts when the girl became pregnant. Worse, the niece had a difficult pregnancy that made it impossible for her to wait on the spoiled spinster hand and foot. When the old lady complained, the niece would say, "Auntie, you can't know how it feels. You've never had a baby."

Finally, the old lady was determined to defeat that argument. She went to the doctor and said, "I'd like you to do something so I can feel what it's like to be pregnant."

"That's impossible," the doctor replied.

"Nonsense," the old lady sputtered. "If you doctors can make an artificial heart, you must be able to let me feel what it's like to carry a baby. Money is no object, I assure you."

The doctor shrugged. "If that's the way you feel, I'll see what I can do." He called the hospital and drove her right over for an operation.

The next day, the spinster calls the doctor from home. "You must be a quack," she complains. "I don't feel pregnant."

"You will," the doctor said. "I sewed your asshole shut."

———————

Just before the funeral services, the undertaker came up to the very elderly widow and asked, "How old was your husband?"

"98," she replied. "Two years older than me."

"So you're 96," the undertaker commented. "Hardly worth going home, isn't it?"

———————

Why do spinsters buy so much soybeans?

They're the perfect meat substitute.

———————

Why was the dirty old man acquitted of the rape charge?

The evidence wouldn't stand up in court.

Did you hear that the Reagan administration is giving out coupons for free food for senior citizens?

Each old person gets five cans of Cycle Four.

———————————

Why do old ladies hire young gigilos instead of looking for love at the Senior Men's Club?

Because at the Senior Men's Club, all the members are wrinkled.

———————————

Why did the old maid commit suicide?

Someone told her marriages are made in heaven.

———————————

An old man went in to see the doctor and said, "Doc, I'm turning eighty tomorrow. I've hired a hooker for the night, and I'd love to do it just one more time before I die. Can you give me something that'll get me up?"

The doctor smiled. "I don't normally prescribe this stuff, but I think in your case I can make an exception for one night."

Later that night, out of curiosity, the doctor phoned the elderly man and asked, "How's it going?"

"Fabulous," the old man said. "I've come three times already."

"That's great," the doctor said. "The hooker must be astounded."

"Not exactly," the old man said. "She's not here yet."

Mrs. Jones hadn't lost a bit of bounce in her seventies, but her husband couldn't begin to get it up. Finally, in desperation, she went to her doctor and described the problem.

The doctor said, "I'll give you a prescription for this miracle drug. Just give your husband three drops a night in his milk before bed."

The old lady thanked him. Two days later, however, she was back in his office dressed in widow's weeds.

"What happened?" the doctor asked.

"By mistake, I gave my husband thirty drops instead of three."

"That's terrible," the doctor said.

"Yes," the widow said. "But my biggest problem right now is, I need an antidote so we can close the coffin."

One old man was sitting on a park bench talking to a new acquaintance. "I'll tell you," he said, "I've learned that arthritis is the cruelest disease."

"Crueler than cancer?" his friend asked.

"You bet," the first codger replied. "It makes every single one of your joints stiff, except the right one."

Did you hear about the new airline for senior citizens?

It's called "Incontinental."

———————————

Why did the 80-year-old man hire a nanny?

Because he loved to be Pampered.

Chapter Nine:

DOUBLY GROSS SEX JOKES

When does a man become a gigilo?

When he's hard up for cash.

How do we know girls aren't made of sugar and spice?

Because they smell like tuna.

The woman had been pregnant for nearly seventeen months when she finally went to see the doctor. The doctor decided to do a Caesarian section. When he cut the woman's abdomen, the baby kicked and screamed and fought like a tiger before the doctor was able to pull him out.

When he cleaned the baby off, the doctor asked, "Why didn't you want to be born after seventeen months?"

"Who wants to come into this lousy world?" the baby replied.

"Why do you have such a terrible opinion of life?" the doctor asked.

"You would too," the baby replied, "if everyone that came in to see you was a prick who threw up on you."

––––––––––––––––

A young couple are undressing on the honeymoon night. The man takes off his pants, tosses them to his bride, and says, "Put those on."

"I can't wear your pants," the girl protests.

"That's right," the husband says arrogantly. "You just remember who wears the pants in this family."

The bride slips off her panties and tosses them to her husband. "Put those on," she says.

He tries to pull them on, but can't even get them over his knees. "I can't get into your pants," he says.

"And you won't," she snaps, "until that male chauvinist attitude of yours changes."

––––––––––––––––

What did the King do when he heard the Queen was screwing the Court Jesters?

He walked in and scared the wits out of her.

One guy nudged another and said, "Who's that very popular girl at the end of the bar?"

The other guy looked, then said, "That's Hurricane Annie."

"Why do you call her 'Hurricane'?"

The second replied, "Because she's a lot more than an ordinary blow."

Why did the guy wear elbow pads to his girl friend's house?

She'd invited him to eat out.

Why did the producer take off his own clothes after he asked the starlet to strip?

He wanted to see if she could make it big.

Deep in the heart of Appalachia, Pa arranges for his youngest son to marry the fourteen-year-old daughter of another backwoods family. He assigns the boy's oldest brother to teach him about sex.

The oldest brother takes the boy out to the woods. He finds a tree with a knothole and starts to teach him the mechanics of making love. Then he tells the boy to practice on his own.

A month later the two clans gather for the wedding. That night, after the party, everybody's sleep is disrupted by an unholy scream. A minute later, the young bride is seen weeping hysterically as she runs to her mother.

Pa turns to his youngest son and angrily asks, "Didn't I get Hank to learn you what to do?"

"I ain't done nothing wrong, Pa," the young boy protested. "Hell, I didn't even get my thing in the knothole. All I did was stick my hand in to check for bees."

What' the world's smallest chicken coop?

A cunt. Only one cock can fit, and it has to stand on its head to get in.

Why should you leave people who masturbate alone?

They're only screwing themselves.

Did you hear about the father who was so unhappy about how his teenage daughter dressed?

He was so disgusted he stopped watching her.

Why do mean hookers suck on ice-cubes?

So they can cold-cock their next customer.

———————

How much does it cost to go to a whorehouse?

Fifty bucks a crack.

———————

A man dies and goes to heaven. While he's waiting to see St. Peter, he notices a gigantic wall covered with clocks. Every once in a while he sees one of the clocks jump ahead fifteen minutes.

Finally, it's his turn to see St. Peter. The first thing he asks is, "What's the story with those clocks?"

"There's a clock for every person on earth," St. Peter replies. "When a man or woman commits adultery, the clock jumps ahead fifteen minutes. That way we can keep track of their sins."

"That's funny," the man says, "I don't see my wife's clock."

"God keeps it in his chamber," St. Peter replies. "He uses it as a fan."

Why did the football team beat off in the huddle?

The coach told them to pull themselves together.

Why wouldn't you want to be an egg?

You only get laid once, it takes five minutes to get hard, you come in a box with eleven other guys, and only your mother sits on your face.

It was orgy time at Plato's Retreat. The very voluptuous blonde was walking around the room, arrogantly inspecting the male merchandise. Finally, she came to a rather scrawny guy in glasses whose equipment was even less impressive than his physique.

The blonde noted his deficiency, then with a smirk asked, "Just who do you expect to please with that?"

"Me," the man replied.

What's the definition of an orgy?

A party where everybody comes.

What's the difference between a porcupine and the Pentagon?

A porcupine has its pricks on the outside.

What's the definition of a fierce competitor?

At a jack-off contest, he finishes first, third, and eighth.

Why are most hookers immune to men?

Because they've been innoculated so many times.

What kind of nymphomaniacs become executive secretaries?

The ones who love desk jobs.

How do you find out who gives the best blow jobs?

You rely on word of mouth.

Two prospectors were about to depart for a long, long winter in the wilds of Alaska. When they stopped at the general store for supplies, the storekeeper, knowing they wouldn't see a woman for more than half a year, presented them with two boards with holes that had fur around them.

The men righteously announced they wouldn't need the boards.

The storekeeper said, "Take them. You can always use them as firewood."

Eight months later, one of the prospectors walked back into the store. "Where's your partner?" the storekeeper asked.

"I shot the bastard," the prospector growled. "I caught him using my board."

———————

A few days after refusing to sleep with her boss, the secretary stormed into his office. "My salary's been cut in half!" she shrieked.

"That's right," the boss replied. "Haven't you ever heard of a withholding tax?"

———————

Did you hear about the guy who borrowed $10,000 from his bank to pay his alimony?

The bank classified it as a "home improvement" loan.

Two widely traveled young women were comparing notes about men. "I like French men the best," one said.

"But French men are domineering and always making cracks about women?" the other protested.

"I know," the first woman said with a smile. "But later they always eat their words."

The voluptuous teenager's mother was always reminding her about what to do if her date tried to park. "A girl's best friend is her legs," the mother would warn.

To the mother's shock, however, her daughter announced she was pregnant.

"How could that happen?" the mother asked. "Haven't I always told you that a girl's best friend is her legs?"

"Yes, mother," the girl said. "But there's always a time when best friends must part."

Why did the guy keep a pubic hair in a matchbook?

As a souvenir of the first time he ate out.

Why do exhibitionists meet at McDonald's?

It's America's favorite take-out place.

135

What comes after 69?

Listerine.

_____

How do you keep your secretary from quitting?

Screw her on the desk.

_____

What's worse than your piano going out of tune before a concert?

Your organ stopping in the middle of a piece.

_____

Why are skilled lovers like mystery writers?

They always come up with a surprising twist at the end.

_____

What do you find under the hood in an Italian car?

A bleach blonde.

Where do you pay in a whorehouse?

At the box office.

———————

Is sex better than drugs?

It depends on the pusher.

———————

Why are cowgirls bow-legged?

Cowboys don't take off their hats when they eat.

———————

How do you know it's really cold outside?

The exhibitionists are describing themselves.

———————

Why was the exhibitionist unhappy after his sex change operation?

He spent $10,000, and he had nothing to show for it.

Why are hookers so unhappy?

Because they're unsuited for their work.

Why are hookers so relentless?

They're attireless workers.

What's foreplay with a fat girl?

Putting up the on and off ramps.

What's a lap dog?

A fat girl who gives head.

When does pot cause castration?

When your girl friend gets the munchies.

Why did the tenor hire a hooker?

He wanted someone to hum his parts.

———————————

What's fellatio foreplay?

A taste of things to come.

———————————

What do cunnilinguists eat in London?

English muffins.

———————————

Why did the woman who was into oral sex buy her husband Gucci underwear?

She believes in putting her money where her mouth is.

———————————

When do women take vibrators to the beach?

When they want to shake and bake.

How does a woman living alone put new zest in her sex life?

She changes the batteries.

Why do married men drink so much?

To see double and feel single.

How can you make your husband an affectionate drunk?

Lace his drinks with rubbing alcohol.

A self-appointed lady killer sauntered confidently up to a young lady at a singles bar and said, "Hi, beautiful. What're the chances of getting into your pants?"

"Not very good," she replied coolly. "One asshole in here is enough."

How do you know a guy's wife is ugly?

When the picture he carries in his wallet is an x-ray.

How do you get even with a guy for coming in your mouth?

Spit it back into his while you kiss.

What's so unusual about cunnilingus?

It's just about the only time a man is content to start at the top and work his way down.

Why did the woman tell her husband she forgot to take her birth control pills?

She wanted him to give her a tongue lashing.

Did you hear they filmed Shakespeare's tragedy "King Lear" as a porno flick?

At the end, there wasn't a dry fly in the house.

What's the difference between a rooster and a nymphomaniac?

The difference between "cock-a-doodle-doo" and "any cock'll do."

———————————

What's a 72?

69 with a 5% meal tax.

———————————

Why did the Democrats recruit nymphomaniacs last November?

They needed enthusiastic pole workers.

———————————

Why did the guy who was into masturbation commit suicide?

He discovered he wasn't his type.

———————————

What's the most famous movie about 69?

"The French Connection."

How do you tell a whimsical masturbator?

By his off-beat sense of humor.

_____

Did you hear about the new prostitutes' union?

Their slogan is, "Look for the union labia."

_____

What do you call a rich man who masturbates?

A self-made millionaire.

_____

What's dangerous about dating a jock?

You could end up with athlete's fetus.

_____

Did you hear about the nearsighted nymphomaniac?

She couldn't recognize her friends until they were on top of her.

Did you hear about the girl who came from a long line of nymphomaniacs?

Her great-great-great-great-great-great-great-great-grandmother came across on the Mayflower.

———————

What's a nymphomaniac's favorite charity?

The sex drive.

———————

What's a flat-chested woman?

One whose baby has to breast feed through a straw.

———————

What's another definition of flat-chested?

When you look down a woman's dress, and the biggest bumps you see are her corns.

———————

How did the female lawyer shock the court?

She dropped her briefs.

Why do female attorneys love trial work?

They're particularly interested in hung juries.

———————————

Do astronauts play badminton in space?

No, but the female astronauts love shuttlecock.

———————————

Where do female astronauts sit in the space shuttle?

In the cuntpit.

———————————

A woman walked into a Washington, D.C. clothing store to buy a bra. The salesman told her, "We have three different kinds—A Democractic bra, a Republican bra, and a liberal bra."

"What's the difference?" the confused woman asked.

"Well," the salesman replied. "The Democratic bra supports the fallen and uplifts the masses. The Republican bra makes mountains out of molehills. And with the liberal bra, your cups runneth over."

What's a real skinny broad?

One who has to have "This side up" tattooed on her chest.

———————————

Why do so many nymphomaniacs suffer from sex insomnia?

They can't keep their thighs closed.

———————————

Why didn't the nymphomaniac visit Mount Rushmore?

She couldn't decide which face to sit on.

———————————

Why are nymphomaniacs so smart?

They're always thinking hard.

———————————

Where do S & M freaks keep their addresses?

In their little black-and-blue books.

Chapter Ten:

DOUBLY DISGUSTING

Why do crabs make a good snack?

You can eat them right out of the box.

_____

How do you know your neighbor has bad acne?

When his Clearasil arrives in 50 gallon drums.

_____

How do you know you have bad acne?

When a pimple breaks, and your Dad claims an oil depletion allowance.

How do you also know when you have bad acne?

When you walk into Pizza Hut and a guy asks if your face is to go.

———————

What's a third sign you have bad acne?

When an Italian tries to squeeze your face over his salad.

———————

What's a foot stool?

A 12 inch shit.

———————

Why are men like public toilets?

They're either taken or full of shit.

———————

What's 6.9?

A good time interrupted by a period.

Did you hear about the abortionist who plea bargained?

They reduced the charges to "child abuse."

———————————

What's the favorite movie of golden shower fetishists?

"I Am Curious, Yellow."

———————————

Did you hear about the abortion clinic that guarantees success?

Their motto is, "No fetus can beat us."

———————————

How do you know a hooker's got bad VD?

When you can't tell her clit from the cankers.

———————————

What should a girl do to stop the wind from messing up her hair?

Shave her ass.

The hooker was delighted when the big handsome stud quickly agreed to "party" with her for $100. But when he started to undress, she angrily said, "Out of here, Buster. You ain't giving me no VD."

"How do you know I have VD?" the man challenged.

"Mac, there ain't many guys your age still wearing Huggies."

———————————

How do you know you're having anal sex with the wrong person?

When her tapeworm bites your dick.

———————————

Why shouldn't you ever drink diet soda after oral sex?

Then you'd have two aftertastes to get out of your mouth.

———————————

Why did the nursery school teacher get fired?

The principal found graffiti on her skirt.

Why is it dangerous to fool around with a married woman who's having her period?

You're likely to get caught red-handed.

————————————

What game do perverted day care workers have their kids play?

Show and smell.

————————————

What should you drink to celebrate your vasectomy?

Dry Sak.

————————————

How can you tell if your kid's nursery school teacher is a child molester?

When your kid brags about giving his teacher a licking.

————————————

Why do child molesters like to work in day care centers?

They like to give little girls and boys a head start.

Did you hear that Gucci is marketing a new laxative?

It's for wealthy people who want to go in style.

―――――――――――

What do you call a gay vampire?

A clot sucker.

―――――――――――

What do you pay a hooker for a golden shower?

The going rate.

―――――――――――

Why is a roadside taco stand like an Exxon station?

At both places people stop in for gas.

―――――――――――

Why did the college student from New Jersey fart in a jar?

So he could open it and take a sniff when he got homesick.

Why is sodomy the easiest kind of sex?

Any ass can do it.

———————————

What do you get if you eat onions and beans?

Tear gas.

———————————

Why should you beware of foreplay with a necrophiliac?

It's murder.

———————————

Why does a necrophiliac have a carefree attitude toward sex?

He doesn't have to worry about birth control.

———————————

What's the worst thing a necrophiliac's wife can say to him?

"Over my dead body."

What did the necrophiliac do when he broke up with his girl friend?

Buried her.

————————

How can you tell a respectful necrophiliac?

He buys black condoms.

————————

What's a necrophiliac's favorite slogan?

Let a hearse put you in the driver's seat.

————————

Why is sex with a golden shower enthusiast so disappointing?

He won't come until you go.

————————

What do you call a child molester who won't attack a 1 year old?

Superstitious.

If you're a gorgeous blonde who's into golden showers, how do you stand on a scale of 1 to 10?

You're-an-8.

―――――――――――

What's a smart cookie?

A guy who peddles Girl Scouts.

―――――――――――

Why don't child molesters like blow jobs?

It's hard to get the bubble gum off their cocks.

―――――――――――

Why do soldiers love to fuck menstruating women?

They love to fight through blood to glory.

―――――――――――

Why did the period fetishist insist his dates use tampons?

So he could floss after eating.

Why do guys use Visine instead of vasoline when their girl friends have their periods?

Visine gets the red out.

What did the kinky college professor say to the coed?

"See you next period."

The usher came up to the woman sitting in the orchestra section at the opera and asked, "Madam, is anyone going to be sitting in that seat next to you?"

"I'm afraid not," she said. "I couldn't get a single one of my friends to come with me."

Knowing the opera had been sold out for months, the usher said, "That's unusual. Why not?"

"This evening, all my friends are at my husband's funeral," she replied.

Why is S&M like charity?

You give 'til it hurts.

What do golden shower enthusiasts shout?

"We're number 1, we're number 1."

_____

What kind of love notes do S&M couples send each other?

Chain letters.

_____

Why doesn't a couple into S&M accept dinner invitations?

They're tied up almost every night.

_____

Did you hear about the racist who was into golden showers?

He went to KKK meetings in a rubber sheet.

_____

What does a child molestor do when he finds a little kid without a penis?

He gives her one.

What did the guy who missed his wife order in the diner?

A vinegar sandwich.

———————————

What's a definition of disgusting?

Beating off into your grandmother's underwear.

———————————

How does a foot fetishist ask for sex?

"Sock it to me!"

———————————

What's a foot fetishist's favorite shoes?

Freudian slippers.

———————————

What does T.G.I.F. mean to a foot fetishist?

Toes Go In First.

A nurse walked into the hospital waiting room and was greeted with an unmistakable stench. "Yuch!" she exclaimed. "Who shit in their pants?"

No one answered the question. Determined to get to the bottom of the odor, she walked around to each patient. Finally, as she approached a drunk in the corner, she knew she had her man.

"Hey," she accused, "how come you didn't answer when I asked who shit in their pants?"

"I thought you meant, who shit in their pants today," the drunk explained.

———————

Why should you take a dead baby along on a cook-out?

You can light it and toast marshmellows.

———————

Why did the S&M loving couple stop parking?

Their cigarette lighter broke.

———————

What's a loser?

A guy who gets VD from a wet dream.

A guy walks into a new diner in his neighborhood to have lunch. He orders a burger, then watches as the waitress goes back into the kitchen. To his dismay, he sees her pick up a handful of chopped meat, thrust it under her armpit, then flap her arm a few times to flatten it.

"Yuch!" he exclaims, turning to the guy on the stool next to him. "Did you see that?"

The other guy shrugged. "That's nothing. If you want disgusting, you ought to be here in the morning when she makes doughnuts."

Why was the dead baby in the kitchen drawer?

They used it to crack nuts.

How do child abusers keep their kids clean?

They bleach them.

Why don't people keep dead babies for long?

They'd end up with a house full of spoiled children.

What's a bad habit?

Scratching your ass.

———————

What's a worse habit?

Scratching your ass and biting your fingernails.

———————

Why do people keep dead babies in the rec room?

They cut off one leg and use it as a ping pong paddle.

———————

Why didn't the guy pay sales tax on the artificial vagina?

He declared it a food item.

———————

What's a vampire's idea of fast food?

A guy with very high blood pressure.

What do child abusers feed their kids after tonsilectomies?

Saltines.

———————————

Why do vampires like their juice fresh-squeezed?

They like to drink it before it clots.

———————————

How do you know you've got bad acne?

When you have to put on your make-up with an ice cream scoop.

———————————

Why was the vampire actress so fussy?

She was waiting for a character she could really sink her teeth into.

———————————

Did you hear about the new book that explains VD to kids?

It's called "I Am Joe's Discharge."

Having sex with a woman who's having her period is a case of mind over matter.

If you don't mind, it doesn't matter.

A woman gets in a cab at the airport and orders the driver to take her home. The meter hits $20 as the cab pulls up in front of the woman's house. She reaches into her purse and to her dismay finds she doesn't have any money.

After a moment's thought, she lifts her skirt up, pulls down her panties, and says to the cab driver, "How about this for my fare."

The cabbie inspects her snatch for a moment, then says, "Lady, you got something smaller?"

Why is piss yellow and semen white?

So guys into golden showers know when they're coming and going.

What do you call it when a guy smokes a joint while getting pissed on?

Mellow yellow.

Why did the cross-eyed foot fetishist have so much trouble with his sex life?

He was always getting off on the wrong foot.

———————

How do you find a convention of golden shower enthusiasts?

Follow the yellow brick road.

———————

What's the definition of a pervert?

A guy who shows up at an orgy with an artificial vagina.

———————

A drunk staggers into a bar and sits down on a stool next to a man and his wife. A moment later, the drunk lets out with a booming and extremely noxious fart.

The man turns to him and angrily says, "How dare you fart before my wife?"

"Gee, I'm sorry," the drunk replied. "I didn't know it was her turn."

How do you know you may be dating a girl with VD?

When you find out she wears prescription underwear.

———————

A traveling salesman called home and asked his wife, "How are the kids?"

"I've got some good news and some bad news," the wife replied. "The bad news is that Joe, Jr. killed his baby sister and cut her up for bait."

"That's horrible!" the husband exclaimed. "What could possibly be the good news?"

"Well," his wife said, "the fish he caught are delicious."

———————

How do you know you have bad acne?

When your little sister plays connect-the-dot on your face.

———————

Why isn't the number 288 used in this book?

It's two gross.

Did you hear that Reagan has decided that Dolly Parton is the solution to the problem of starvation in Africa?

He's sending her over to breast-feed Ethiopia.

Are a lot of Congressmen into S&M?

So many that they've appointed a House Whip.

How do you know a guy's wife is ugly?

When his pet name for her is "Rover."

How do you tell an Ethiopian Jew?

He's the stick with the Rolex on his wrist.

How do you know your kid is fat?

After he gets off a merry-go-round, they have to shoot the horse.

What's Ethiopian sex?

A dry hump.

How do you know your parents hate you?

When they put a live teddy bear in your crib.

Why do such a high percentage of men get elected to public office?

Because women are split.

How do you know your son's a future Nazi?

When you find him in the john beating off to Sargeant Slaughter comics.

How do you know your kid is ugly?

When you have to hang a pork chop around his neck so the dog will play with him.

A woman went next door to find the neighbor woman looking haggard and worn. "What's wrong?" she asked.

The woman grimaced. "Billy pushed his sister into the well two days ago," she replied.

"That's awful."

"It sure is. Now we have to sterilize our water."

The television network interrupted its prime time programming with the following bulletin:

"Earth received bad news and good news just hours ago. The bad news is that our planet has been invaded by Martians. The good news is that they eat politicians and pee gasoline."

Have you heard about the new "2 Week LSD Diet?"

You take just two tablets and you lose 14 days.

Why is it so cheap to build a house in Ethiopia?

Houses don't need to have kitchens.

What is Germany doing to help solve the starvation problem in Ethiopia?

They've shipped out a dozen of their largest ovens.

———————————

What's the fastest animal in the world?

A chicken in Ethiopia.

———————————

What do Ethiopians and Yoko Ono have in common?

They both live off of dead beatles.

———————————

Why have the South Africans imported a planeload of Ethiopians with swollen feet?

They use them as three-woods.

The widow was standing by the coffin of her husband while the mourners filed past. The third man stopped and said, "Mrs. Jones, your husband looks so serene. What did he die of?"

The wife said, "The poor man died of gonorrhea."

The startled man moved on. A few minutes later, a woman asked, "How did the late Mr. Jones meet his end?"

The widow again said, "He died of gonorrhea."

After the woman passed, the widow's son, who'd been standing behind her, finally stepped forward and said, "Mother, I can't listen to this any more. You know Dad died of diarrhea, not gonorrhea. Why are you saying that terrible thing?"

"Because," the widow replied, "I'd rather have people think he died like a sport, instead of like the shit he was all his life."

———————

How do you know your daughter is ugly?

When she goes to a stag party and men want to play dress poker.

———————

What's a miscarriage?

Love's labors lost.

What's a hysterectomy?

An operation that removes the baby carriage but leaves the playpen in good condition.

———————

Why did the space shuttle explode?

There were two cracks in the Challenger.

———————

Did the five male astronauts enjoy having two women aboard the Challenger?

They had a blast.

———————

Why didn't Christa McAullife and Judith Resnick make good astronauts?

After lift-off, they just went to pieces.

———————

What's the first thing President Regan did after the space shuttle blew up?

Appointed an all-black crew for the next flight.

What did NASA change first when the Challenger exploded?

They took the "Orbit or Bust" signs off the other shuttles.

**Mysteries from the
Masters of Suspense**

By Sax Rohmer

DAUGHTER OF FU MANCHU   (1818, $3.50)

THE DRUMS OF FU MANCHU   (1617, $3.50)

THE INSIDIOUS DR. FU MANCHU   (1668, $3.50)

THE TRAIL OF FU MANCHU   (1619, $3.50)

SHADOW OF FU MANCHU   (1870, $3.50)

By John Dickson Carr

THE MAN WHO COULD NOT SHUDDER (1703, $3.50)

THE PROBLEM OF THE WIRE CAGE   (1702, $3.50)

THE EIGHT OF SWORDS   (1881, $3.50)

THE SURVIVALIST SERIES
by Jerry Ahern

TALES OF TERROR AND POSSESSION
from Zebra Books

HALLOWEEN II   (1080, $2.95)
by Jack Martin
The terror begins again when it is Halloween night in Haddonfield, Illinois. Six shots pierce the quiet of the normally peaceful town—and before night is over, Haddonfield will be the scene of yet another gruesome massacre!

MAMA   (1247, $3.50)
by Ruby Jean Jensen
Once upon a time there lived a sweet little dolly, but her one beaded glass eye gleamed with mischief and evil. If Dorrie could have read her doll's thoughts, she would have run for her life—for her dear little dolly only had killing on her mind.

WAIT AND SEE   (1857, $3.95)
by Ruby Jean Jensen
"Don't go near the river," Kevin's aunt had said. But something dark and evil was waiting for him there, beckoning to him. Something that once freed, would exact a terrifying, unthinkable revenge.

ROCKINGHORSE   (1743, $3.95)
by William W. Johnstone
It was the most beautiful rockinghorse Jackie and Johnny had ever seen. But as they took turns riding it they didn't see its lips curve into a terrifying smile. They couldn't know that their own innocent eyes had taken on a strange new gleam.

JACK-IN-THE-BOX   (1892, $3.95)
by William W. Johnstone
Any other little girl would have cringed in horror at the sight of the clown with the insane eyes. But as Nora's wide eyes mirrored the grotesque wooden face her pink lips were curving into the same malicious smile.

Available wherever paperbacks are sold, or order direct from the Publisher. Send cover price plus 50¢ per copy for mailing and handling to Zebra Books, Dept. 1945, 475 Park Avenue South, New York, N.Y. 10016. Residents of New York, New Jersey and Pennsylvania must include sales tax. DO NOT SEND CASH.

THE OMNI COLLECTION
from Zebra Books

THE OMNI BOOK OF SPACE (1275, $3.95)
Edited by Owen Davies
The OMNI BOOK OF SPACE offers 35 articles by some of the best known writers of our time, including Robert Heinlein, James Michener, and Ray Bradbury, which offer a guide to the research and engineering that can make our world a better place to live.

**THE OMNI BOOK OF COMPUTERS
AND ROBOTS** (1276, $3.95)
Edited by Owen Davies
They have become a part of our lives: at work and at home computers are being used more and more, and every day we see more evidence of the computer revolution. This fascinating book is available to answer all the questions and unravel the mystery.

THE OMNI BOOK OF MEDICINE (1364, $3.95)
Edited by Owen Davies
A life span of two hundred years? A world without pain? These medical advances — and many more — are right around the corner and are part of this remarkable collection of articles that will give you a glimpse of a healthier tomorrow.

THE OMNI BOOK OF PSYCHOLOGY (1868, $3.95)
Edited by Peter Tyson
Dreams, mind control, psychographics — these are the topics that can both excite and frighten all of us when we think about the techniques of psychology in the future. In this volume you will see how the barriers of human fear and high-tech anxiety will be broken.

**THE OMNI BOOK OF HIGH-TECH
SOCIETY 2000** (1896, $3.95)
Edited by Peter Tyson
In a world of computer revolutions, new biomedical frontiers and alternative energy sources, where will you stand? You can match wits with Arthur C. Clarke by taking the quiz included in this book. Welcome to the future!